WHEN NANTUCKET MEN WENT WHALING

in 1810, the whaling industry was at its peak. Here is the authentic and dramatic story of the men and their families whose way of life was shaped by this unusual industry.

Based on firsthand source material from old logs, diaries, and journals, actual people and actual places are realistically portrayed in this exciting narrative. Real whalers bravely face the dangers of huge whales and unknown seas in their tiny boats, real families at home live their daily lives, real sights, smells, and busy scenes take place on the wharves and on shipboard—all of these and more come alive for young readers. The text is further enlivened by lovely old prints and engravings and by illustrations.

This book is one of a group called *How They Lived* being developed by Garrard to give meaning to the study of American history. Our nation's strength and growth are based upon unique contributions of many kinds of people from all parts of the country. The books will give young people a deeper understanding and appreciation of history and geography as they see life in the past through the eyes of the people who lived it.

When Nantucket Men Went Whaling

GARRARD PUBLISHING COMPANY

CHAMPAIGN, ILLINOIS

When Nantucket Men Went Whaling

BY ENID LaMONTE MEADOWCROFT

ILLUSTRATED BY VICTOR MAYS

This book is for

James Milton O'Neill III

who loves to fish and would, I'm sure,

go whaling if he could

Brown Brothers: p. 54, 88
Culver Pictures, Inc.: p. 11, 55, 87
Harvard College Library, Dept. of Printing and Graphic Arts: p. 28
The Marine Historical Association, Inc., Mystic Seaport, Mystic, Conn.: p. 41 (bottom), 43
The Mariners Museum, Newport News, Va.: p. 24–25
Nantucket Historical Association, Nantucket, Mass.: p. 1, 89, back cover
New York Public Library Picture Collection: p. 5, 13, 21, 23, 26, 38–39, 44, 51
Harry Shaw Newman, Old Print Shop, N.Y.: p. 2, 3, 14, 68, 84–85, 92
Nimrod of the Sea, by William Morris Davis (New York: Harper and Brothers, 1874): p. 74, 75
Peabody Museum of Salem, Mass.: p. 91
Whaling Museum, New Bedford, Mass.: p. 41 (top), 42, 93
Arthur Griffin: Endsheets

Contents

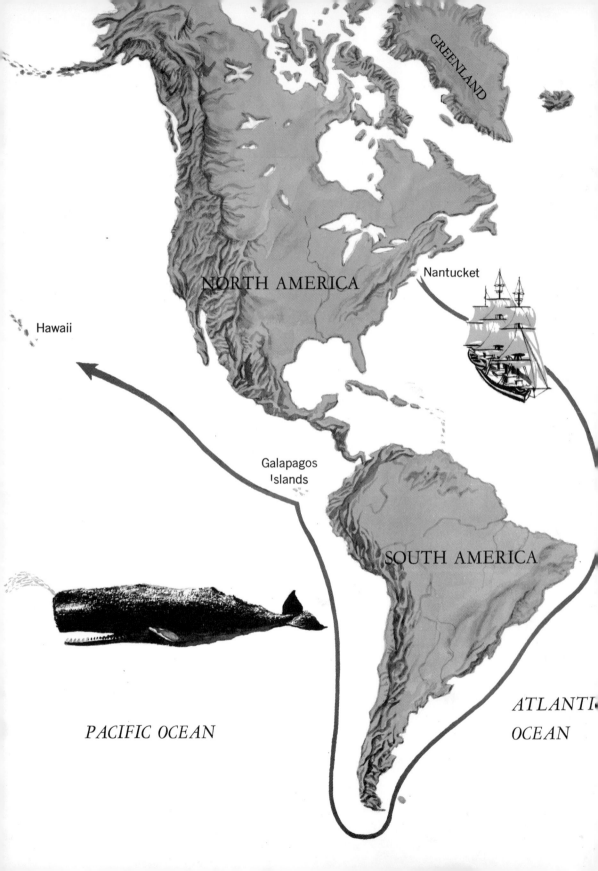

GREENLAND

NORTH AMERICA

Nantucket

Hawaii

Galapagos
Islands

SOUTH AMERICA

PACIFIC OCEAN

*ATLANTIC
OCEAN*

1. A Dead Whale
and a Stove Boat

**"Oh, the rare old whale,
  Mid storm and gale,
  In his ocean home will be."**

On a fine day in March 1810, Captain Peleg Brown stood at the bow of his little whaling ship *Betsy*, gazing out over the Pacific Ocean. For two stormy days he and his crew had been cruising about, looking for whales, and not a whale had they seen.

Now the sea was calm and a fair wind filled the *Betsy's* dingy sails. Several men of her crew were at work on the deck. One man was sharpening long-handled cutting spades on the big grindstone near the hatchway. Another was splicing a rope. Two men were mending sails, using thick needles and heavy twine.

The cooper, or barrel-maker, was repairing a greasy oil cask. The cabin boy was scouring a large iron pot with a piece of sharkskin. And high on his perch near the top of the foremost mast, the lookout scanned the sea.

Suddenly, off in the distance, the lookout saw a column of white mist shoot up into the air.

"She blows!" he shouted. "To starboard! A mile off! She blows! She bl-o-o-o-ws!"

Captain Brown spotted the whale through his spyglass.

"Call all hands!" he cried. "Get ready to lower the boats!"

The men sprang to obey. Two small whale-boats were quickly lowered into the water with a splash. Scrambling over the side of the ship, six men took their places in each boat. Soon they were rowing toward the whale.

The first mate sat in the stern of one boat, steering it with a long, heavy oar. The second mate steered the other. The captain, the cook, the cabin boy, and the cooper had stayed aboard the ship.

The whaleboats were light and only twenty-seven feet long, but they were strong enough to ride the roughest waves. These boats carried cutting spades, lances, and harpoons. There were also two strong ropes, or lines, in each boat. Each line was carefully coiled in its own wooden tub.

Only the boat steerers faced forward. The other men rowed, their backs to the whale. They did not look around for fear of spoiling their stroke. Soon they could hear the whale spouting.

The huge black monster spouted lazily. Then it sank below the surface and rose to spout again. Its tiny eyes were set in each side of its tremendous head, and it could not see the boats coming up behind it.

"Steady," said the first mate in a low voice to his men. "Stand by your iron, harpooner."

The man in the bow laid down his oar and stood up. He moved quietly, for whales have keen hearing. If they are startled by sudden noises, they may sound, or dive down deep, and swim away.

Quietly the harpooner picked up a long heavy harpoon. It was fastened to a line in one of the tubs and was used like a fishhook.

Harpooners, holding their irons, stand ready to hurl them as the whaleboats come up behind a sperm whale.

The harpooner turned around. The whale was only a few feet from the boat, still blind to its danger.

"Let him have it!" commanded the first mate.

With all his force the harpooner darted his iron into the great black body. Then, like a flash, he hurled the second harpoon, which was attached to the same line.

The startled whale leaped in pain and plunged into the ocean, headfirst. As it went down, its huge tail thrashed about in the air.

"Stern all!" yelled the second mate to his crew. "Stern all!"

Hastily the second mate's crew tried to back away, but the whale's big fan-like tail hit the side of their boat with a crash. Men, lances, harpoons, cutting spades, oars, and broken planks were tossed into the water.

The first mate and his men did not cut their line so that they could help the second mate and his crew. Their job was to get the whale.

For several minutes it swam about madly under water, pulling their boat this way and that. Then it rose some distance away and raced across the sea, dragging the little boat behind it.

The men put up their oars and clung to their seats. Up and over the waves they went, through showers of cold, salty spray. They leaned to one side and the other so that the boat would not capsize, as the whale zigzagged here and there, trying to escape.

The whale swam on rapidly for several miles. Then it grew tired and swam more slowly. Soon it was barely moving.

"Haul in!" the first mate commanded quietly. The men hauled on the line which was attached to the harpoons in the whale's body. They pulled their boat so close to the exhausted whale that they could almost touch it.

This whaleboat, pulled by a harpooned whale, races through the sea on a "Nantucket sleigh ride."

By this time the first mate and the harpooner had changed places. The first mate raised a long, sharp lance. He plunged it into the whale's body at a spot over the lungs. The whale spouted blood and leaped out of the water. Quickly the mate cut the line fastened to the harpoons, and the men backed their boat away. The whale thrashed about and swam around in circles, beating the water into bloody foam with its tail. At last it died.

Then the first mate cut a hole in the huge jaw with a cutting spade and fastened a line through the hole. The men rowed slowly back to the ship, towing the dead whale behind them.

This was a long, hard, back-breaking task which took them several hours. It was nearly dark when they reached the ship. The second mate and his crew had been rescued by the captain and the cooper. One of the men had broken his leg, and Captain Brown had set it in splints. The other men helped lash the great whale to the side of the ship. When this was finished, the men went below to their quarters.

This may not be exactly how the whale was caught by men from the *Betsy* on that day long ago. All we know surely is how whales were hunted and what one of those men wrote in his journal that night.

His name was Silas Bunker. Here is what he wrote:

"Thurs. Mar. 4, 1810. Rough weather and no whales for two days. Saw one today at 1 P M and gave chase. At 7 P M got him back to ship. 2nd mate's boat stove in. Poor Ben got his leg broke. Whale should make 90 barrels good oil. 300 more barrels to fill. Then off for home."

Home for all the men aboard the *Betsy* was the island of Nantucket, nearly halfway around the world.

2. The Faraway Island

Nantucket is a small island in the Atlantic Ocean. It lies about thirty miles south of Cape Cod and is part of Massachusetts.

Long ago, the island belonged to the Indians. They named it Nantucket which means "faraway island." Sometimes they told their children this story about a giant who used Cape Cod for his bed.

"One night the giant could not sleep," they said. "He tossed around so much that his moccasins became filled with sand. Angrily he took them off and flung them far away into the ocean. One of them became Nantucket."

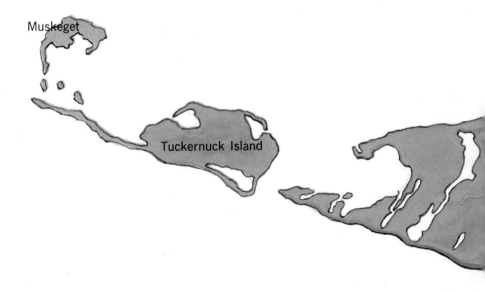

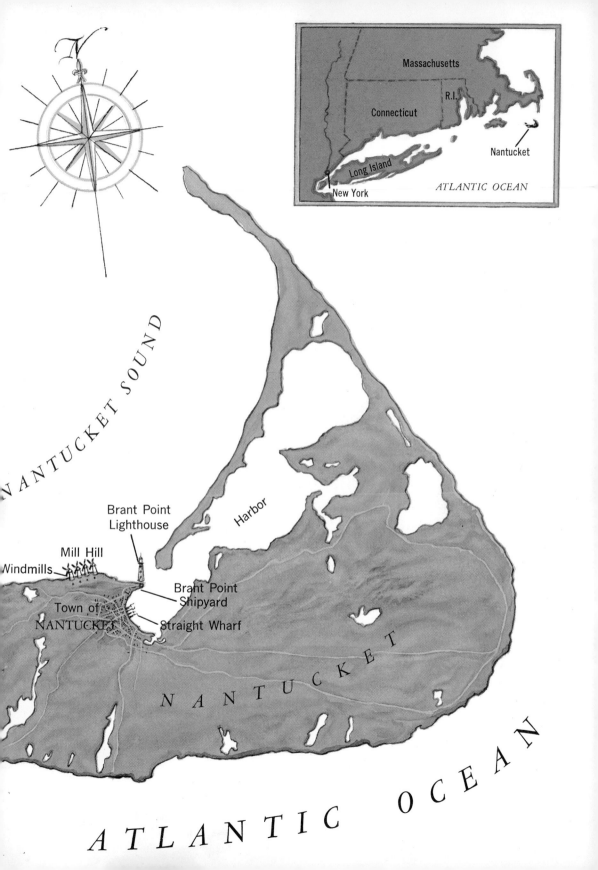

N

Massachusetts

Connecticut

R.I.

Nantucket

Long Island

New York

ATLANTIC OCEAN

NANTUCKET SOUND

Brant Point
Lighthouse

Harbor

Mill Hill

Windmills

Brant Point
Shipyard

Town of
NANTUCKET

Straight Wharf

N A N T U C K E T

ATLANTIC OCEAN

The Indians lived alone on Nantucket until 1659. Then a white man from Massachusetts, named Thomas Macy, sailed to the island with his family and settled there.

The Indians were friendly. More people came from the colony of Massachusetts and the settlement grew. The men hunted, fished, raised sheep, and farmed. The women spun, wove, and cared for their families. The children helped with the work. When they weren't busy, they roamed the beaches. They dug for clams and watched the whales which often swam about near the island.

One day a small whale swam right into the harbor. People ran down to the shore to see it. The whale played about for three days. Finally, some of the men decided to kill it, for they had learned from the Indians that whale fat, or blubber, makes good oil. Just how they killed it, no one knows. More than a hundred years ago, one man in Nantucket wrote this about it:

"They accordingly invented and caused to be wrought for them a harpoon, with which they attacked and killed the whale."

When the whale was dead, the men towed it to shore. Then they dragged it up on the sand

and hacked off big hunks of blubber. Meanwhile, other men made a hot fire on the beach and hung a large iron pot over it.

The blubber was put into the pot. It sizzled and crackled as it melted to oil. Black smoke rose in clouds and the smell of the boiling oil was terrible. Even when it was cool, the oil smelled bad. But the settlers were glad to have it. They gave some to their wives to be used in their lamps at home and sold the rest.

Some people think that the Indians helped the settlers kill the whale and try out the fat. Again, no one really knows. But one thing is sure. From that time on, Nantucket men chased whales.

Whales are not fish. They are mammals and must have air or they will die. They breathe through nostrils on top of their heads, and hold their breath while they swim under water. Then they come to the surface and blow out tall, misty columns of air. This spouting helps the whale hunters to find them.

Whales are warm-blooded like the land animals. The thick layers of blubber under their skins protect them from the cold. The blubber oil was used for many years to light homes, shops, and streets. It was also used for curing leather and for making wool easy to card.

Some whales are small, like the porpoises. Others are larger than the largest dinosaur that ever lived. Whales have been caught which have weighed over a hundred tons, or more than sixty large elephants might weigh.

It took great courage for the men of Nantucket to go out after these huge creatures in small boats. At first they chased only the whales they could see from the shore, and tried out their blubber on the beach. Then they built larger, stronger boats with try-pots on the decks, and sailed far from home, hunting whales.

They sailed around Cape Horn at the tip of South America and into the Pacific Ocean.

They cruised about on the South Seas. They made their way along the coast of Africa, around the Cape of Good Hope, and into the Indian Ocean. They battled snow and ice off the coast of Greenland.

Wherever they went, they hunted two kinds of whales. They were called right whales and sperm whales.

Sperm Whale

Right Whale

Peter Folger, who went whaling on the sloop *Greyhound* in 1753, wrote about the right whale in his journal.

"A Right whale is very large," he wrote, "hollowing on the back, all slick and smooth, having no hump at all as other Whales. The bone (of which is made stays and hooped petticoats) doth grow in their mouth. The tongue is monstrous large and will commonly make a tun of oyl."

Sperm whales made tons of oil, too. It was better than the oil that right whales yielded. And the enormous heads of sperm whales contained a waxy stuff called spermaceti which made excellent candles.

In a Boston newspaper, printed over two hundred years ago, an advertisement appeared:

"For sale: Sperma-Ceti candles, exceeding all others for Beauty, Sweetness of Scent when extinguished. Duration more than double Tallow Candles of Equal Size. Size of Flames nearly four times more."

Of course, many Americans wanted spermaceti candles and whale oil for their lamps. So did many people in Europe. The people living on Nantucket supplied both.

Wax is melted and poured into candle molds in an early American candlemaker's shop. The man on the right is dipping candle wicks into liquid wax.

Thousands of candles were molded in their small candle factories every year. Great quantities of whale oil were cleaned and refined in their tryhouses. Nantucket merchants shipped oil and candles to Boston, New York, Philadelphia, Charleston, and across the Atlantic Ocean to cities in England, France, and Spain.

By 1810, when the men aboard the *Betsy* were hunting whales in the Pacific, almost every family on Nantucket depended on whaling for a living. And the little town of Nantucket was the whaling center of the world.

1

2

3

4

5

6

7

These old prints show the many uses of whale products in the great days of the whaling industry. (1) stripping blubber; (2) whale oil for lighthouses; (3) oil for lamps; (4) manufacturing of whale oil; (5) fertilizer from whale by-products; (6) cooking blubber for food; (7) whalebone in clothing and umbrellas; (8) fine perfume made from ambergris, another product of whales.

8

3. Greasy Luck

" 'A sail! A sail!' How rang the sound
  Through old Nantucket's humble homes!
  We knew our ship was homeward bound
  And now at last perhaps she comes!"

On June 3, 1810, a grimy, oil-blackened whaling ship made her way toward Nantucket. No record tells us what time she reached the island. Perhaps it was in the afternoon. It was on a Sunday, and the day probably began like any other Sunday in June.

Breakers pounded against the beaches with a dull roar. Sandpipers skittered along the water's edge, searching for insects. Sea gulls screamed harshly as they swooped low, looking for fish.

Ships with furled sails swung at anchor in the harbor. Smaller vessels, which were moored on one side of each of the four long wharves, rocked gently on the waves. The shops and sail lofts on the opposite sides of the wharves were closed. So were the ships and warehouses along the waterfront. In the town everything was quiet.

The town nestled on a low hill near the harbor. Small, gray, shingled houses clustered along the sandy, winding roads. Here and there, a house had been painted red or white, and a larger house stood a little apart from its neighbors.

Many of the houses had railed platforms on the roofs, called walks. From these walks, shipowners and whalers' wives could watch for home-coming ships.

West of the town, on Mill Hill, there were four windmills for grinding corn, and a tall lookout tower. East of the town, on Brant Point, which jutted into the ocean, there was a lighthouse. The rest of the island was country, with scattered farmhouses, pasture-land, a common where sheep grazed, some ponds, and salt marshes.

Although it was Sunday, people rose early.

In town, two herdsmen walked through the streets, blowing their horns. Boys ran to the barns or sheds behind their homes to let out the cows, which the herdsmen collected and drove out to pasture. Then the boys hauled buckets of water from the wells and carried bundles of peat or armloads of wood into their mothers' kitchens.

Meanwhile, in many kitchens, women were cooking breakfast over their open fires. In most houses the kitchen was the living room and dining room, too. There was usually a loom in one corner and a spinning wheel nearby. Pewter dishes gleamed in the cupboard.

Busy housewives tidy their backyards in this view of Nantucket painted by Phoebe Folger in 1797-1806.

Pots and pans hung in orderly rows on the fireplace and there was a kettle hanging on the crane over the hearth.

In some homes Sunday breakfast was fish chowder. In others it was corn-meal mush or bean porridge. Often the food was cooked on Saturday night and warmed up on Sunday in big iron pots.

By the time the meal was over and the household chores were done, church bells had begun to ring.

In 1810 more than half the people on Nantucket Island were Quakers. They dressed in sober grays and browns. The women wore long, full skirts, cloaks or shawls, and big bonnets. The men wore homespun suits, broad-brimmed hats, and buckles on their square-toed shoes.

The children dressed like their parents. They were supposed to behave like them, too. But it must have been hard, on a fine June morning, to walk sedately along the sandy roads, with the sea gulls crying and the whitecaps on the ocean dancing in the sun.

There were few fathers or older brothers there to keep the children in order. For many men and older boys were far away whaling,

and others had been lost at sea. Quaker
mothers were kind and gentle, but they were
strict. So the children sat quietly through the
long Quaker meeting. Perhaps they were
thinking of what they would have for dinner.

There might be a crusty meat pie, baked
in the oven which was built into one side of
the fireplace. Or a chicken or duck, roasted on
a spit over the coals. In June the vegetables
in the garden were not yet ready to eat. But
there would be potatoes, parsnips, or turnips
which had been stored in cellars all winter.

There would be plenty of milk, too, with
homemade bread and freshly churned butter.

And for dessert there would be custard, or pudding, or pie made from dried apples or berries.

After dinner on Sunday, which the Quakers called First Day, most of the children were kept quietly at home. But a few boys always went to the watchtower on Mill Hill. There they waited, hoping that the lookout in the tower might spy an approaching ship. And, of course, on June 3, 1810, he did. He could not yet make out her name, even through his spyglass. But he called down his news to the boys and one of them ran to the home of the town crier.

Soon the crier was walking up the main street, ringing his bell.

"A ship is coming," he cried. "No name yet. A ship is coming! A ship!"

The news spread quickly from house to house. People with walks hurried up the narrow stairs to their attics and climbed through the scuttles to watch the ship approach. Others hastened to Mill Hill.

The whaling ship drew nearer. Women prayed silently that she might be the one on which their husbands or sons had sailed. Excited children hoped that she was bringing

home their fathers. Old whaling men watched
her coming closer and smiled. She was riding
low in the water. That meant that her hold
was filled with casks of whale oil.

"They've had greasy luck," the old whaling
men said. "It's been a good voyage. They've
had greasy luck."

In the tower, the lookout was squinting
through his glass.

"She's the *Ranger*," he called out at last.
"Captain William Joy."

Like shots from a gun, several boys raced
off to Captain Joy's house. For the first boy
to carry the news to a captain's family that

his ship had been sighted, was always given
a new silver dollar.

On came the *Ranger* with her dingy sails
billowing in the breeze. She was so heavily
loaded that she could not cross the bar of
sand which stretched under water across the
entrance of the harbor. So her men dropped
anchor outside the bar and rowed ashore in
their whaleboats.

An eager little crowd waited on the wharf
to greet those brawny, sun-tanned whalers.
Wives welcomed their husbands and mothers
welcomed their sons with joyful faces.
Children were a little shy at first with fathers

they hardly knew. Other relatives and friends gathered around the whalers and walked with them to their homes.

The whaling men had been gone for nearly two years. They were anxious for news and so were their families. There was much to talk about as women prepared good meals for the men who had eaten ship's food for so long.

In the evening, friends and neighbors stopped in to visit, and stayed until the town bell rang at nine o'clock. This was the curfew bell, warning the people that they should all be in their own homes.

If there was no moon, the town was dark. Nantucket oil lighted the streets of many cities in America and Europe, but not the streets of Nantucket.

"Why use oil so foolishly when we can sell it?" asked the thrifty Nantucketers. So the home-goers carried lanterns.

When the visitors had left, sleepy children lighted their candles, and climbed the stairs to their beds under the eaves. Soon they were sleeping soundly between homespun sheets, under patchwork quilts. And at last the grownups banked their fires, blew out their whale oil lamps, and went to bed, too.

4. Sea Chests
and Other Things

The next morning the work of unloading the *Ranger* began. Men in broad-decked sloops, called lighters, sailed out to the whaling ship. One after another, they hoisted the greasy casks of sperm oil from the *Ranger's* hold. Then they put them aboard their lighters.

When each lighter had a full load, her crew sailed her over the bar, across the harbor, to Straight Wharf. There the casks were rolled up the gangplank to the dock and onto drays.

Some of them were drayed to a big warehouse at the head of the wharf. Others were taken to a tryhouse nearby, where oil was refined before it was sold.

The *Ranger* had brought home 1,800 barrels of oil. Another ship, the *John Jay*, with 1,400 casks aboard, was being lightened at the same time. Lighter-men called back and forth as they struggled with the heavy casks. Dray drivers shouted at their horses. Hoofs clattered and wheels rumbled over the wooden wharf.

The three other wharves were noisy, too, for

little schooners were constantly coming and going. Dock hands were loading boxes of candles and barrels of oil on outbound schooners. Incoming schooners were bringing lumber from Maine, barrels of pitch and tar from North Carolina, bars of iron from Connecticut, firewood from New Hampshire, and groceries from Boston and New York.

The wharves were piled high with boxes, barrels, crates, and bags. Some of the merchandise which was brought to the island would go to homes on Nantucket. But most of it was to be used on the whaling ships.

In the little shops and lofts on the wharves and along the waterfront, men were busy making things for those ships.

Forges glowed and hammers clanged in the blacksmith shops, as smiths beat out harpoons, lances, chains, cutting spades, and blubber hooks. In the coopers' shops, some men sat astride wooden shaving horses, making barrel staves. Others fitted iron hoops to half-finished casks.

Sailmakers were cutting sails from yards of canvas laid out on the floors of the sail lofts, or sewing them together with strong needles and stout twine. In each of several long buildings, called rope walks, one man turned a big wheel, spinning hemp into strands of yarn. Another walked backwards, away from the wheel, twisting the yarn into rope.

These old etchings show how coopers made barrels, used to store whale oil.

Every man, no matter what he was making, was doing his best. For he knew that the success of a whaling voyage depended in some way on his work. Whalers must have stout sails, strong ropes, sharp harpoons and lances, and tight casks if they were to bring home oil. And oil was important to all the people on Nantucket.

At noon the town bell rang, calling the workmen home to dinner. School children went home for dinner, too. The children of Captain William Joy and the other whalers from the *Ranger* probably ran all the way. They would hurry to see their fathers, and also to find out if the whalers' sea chests had been brought from the ship.

Every whaling man had a sea chest. It was like a small flat-topped trunk. His family usually gathered around him eagerly when he unpacked it.

First, out would come his clothes, stiff with salt and stained with oil. There were blue pea

jackets and striped cotton shirts. There were wool trousers, duck trousers, stockings, long woolen underwear, shoes, and caps.

Clothes wore out quickly at sea and the whalers did their own mending. Sometimes they sewed ragged red woolen drawers inside old trousers which had holes in the seat or knees. They stitched torn shirts and worn-out jackets together, too. Then they put on patches, if they were needed. They patched their clothes so often that sailors used to say, "You'll know a whaling man wherever you see him, because of his patches."

Surely some wives smiled when those funny-looking garments were taken out of the sea chests. But the children would watch impatiently to see the gifts which were packed in with the clothes.

There was always scrimshaw. This was the name given to things which whalers carved from the big ivory teeth and the jawbones of whales, and then decorated.

In their spare time aboard ship, they made ivory dominoes, jackstraws, and little animals for their children. They carved fancy rolling pins, butter paddles, and jagging wheels, used to crimp the edges of pies, for their wives.

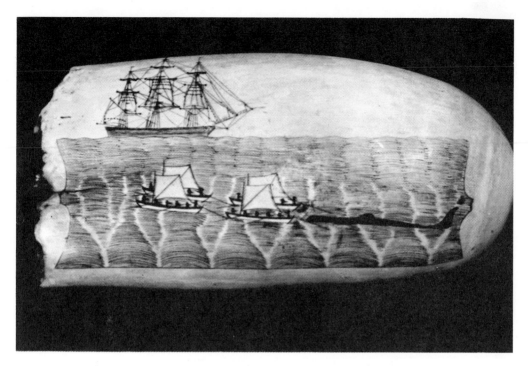

An engraved whale's tooth (above) shows a captured whale being towed to the ship. A ditty box (below) was used by whalers to hold sewing supplies.

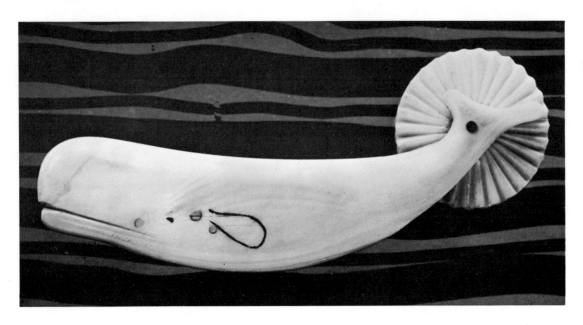

This is an example of later, more polished scrimshaw.

They engraved pictures on teeth and pieces
of bone, to be used as ornaments in their
homes, or to give to the girls they hoped to
marry. They made penholders, inkwells,
bracelets, cane handles, yarn winders and many
other things. Some of them can still be seen
today in whaling museums. And in 1810 there
was probably not a family on Nantucket which
did not own a piece of scrimshaw.

Most whalers brought home other presents,
too. These came from places where their ship
had stopped for fresh supplies. One man might

have a war club from Madagascar, wrapped in a shirt. Another might bring back a fierce-looking mask from Tasmania, tucked under some trousers.

Men who had been to Tahiti in the South Seas would bring home beautiful shells and pink coral. And those who had landed in Australia might have small models of war canoes, which had been carved by the natives.

This scrimshaw and the fish on page 42 are jagging wheels used for decorating pies and cakes.

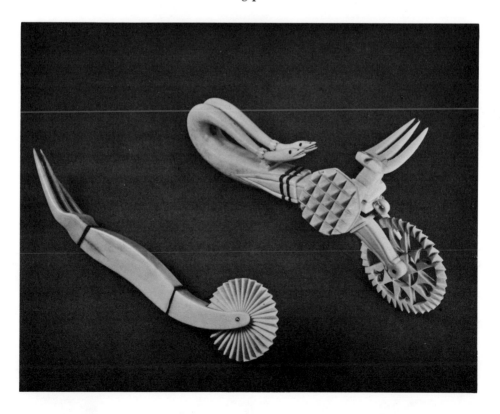

Sometimes there were gifts which could not travel in sea chests, like chattering gray monkeys, or green and blue parrots, or cages of little bright-colored birds. One whaler even brought home a tortoise from the Galapagos Islands which was so large his children could ride on it.

No one knows what presents Captain Joy and the crew of the *Ranger* brought to their families. But we can be sure that their wives and children were glad to get them, and gladder still to have the men safe at home for a while.

5. A Busy Morning
for Zenas Coffin

"Old Uncle Pillick, he built him a boat
 On the ba-a-ck side of Nantucket P'int.
 He rolled up his trousers and set her afloat
 From the ba-a-ck side of Nantucket P'int."

Captain Zenas Coffin was not building his own boat, like Uncle Pillick in the old Nantucket song. He was having three new whaleboats built for him in the shipyard on Brant Point.

Captain Coffin belonged to an old whaling family. There were so many Coffins on Nantucket that it was hard for anyone to keep track of them. The Coffin boys usually shipped aboard whalers as cabin boys when they were thirteen or fourteen years old. If they were not killed in a whaling accident or lost at sea, most of them rose to become captains.

Zenas Coffin had been the captain of four ships. After several years at sea, he had given up whaling to stay with his family. Now he was one of the richest men on the island. He and his brothers owned the *John Jay* and five other whaling ships. They also owned the big warehouse at the head of Straight Wharf, a tryhouse and a candle factory.

The tryhouse was a long shed where oil from the whaling ships was refined. Fires burned hotly under great kettles. Oil bubbled and smoked as workmen with long-handled ladles skimmed off bits of blubber which came to the surface. When the oil was clean, it was put into tubs and left until the winter's cold had turned it partly solid.

Then it was shoveled into bags which were squeezed in a big press. Fine clear oil spurted out of the bags into new casks. If it was oil from a sperm whale, a yellowish material was left in the bags. This was taken to the candle factory and made into spermaceti candles.

46

The Coffins' ships brought home plenty of oil. Their warehouse was almost bursting with rows of casks, boxes of candles, bundles of whalebone, and things which had been bought in foreign lands with money made by whaling.

Zenas Coffin lived with his wife and six children on Pine Street in one of the largest houses in Nantucket. It had eight rooms with a fireplace in each room. Behind the house was a stable where Captain Coffin kept three horses and a small, two-wheeled carriage, in which he and Mrs. Coffin sometimes went for a ride. A hired man, named Warren Bump, took care of the horses and of Captain Coffin's big farm, near the south shore.

Mrs. Coffin and her three daughters did the housework and looked after two younger boys. Nine-year-old Charles was often with his father.

One morning late in June, they went together to see how the new whaleboats were coming along. It was a beautiful day, with the water beyond Brant Point sparkling in the sun. Boys were swimming near the lighthouse at the end of the point, or fishing from rowboats.

The shipyard lay along the shore between the lighthouse and the town. Whaling ships were not built on the island in 1810. But carpenters were busy repairing schooners, which had been pulled up on the beach, and working on half-finished whaleboats.

The boats stood on ways, or beds of blocks, set up on the hard, wet sand near the shore line. Each boat was made of strong, light cedar boards, half an inch thick. Since whaleboats were used for hard work in rough seas, it was necessary to have new boats built for every voyage. There were several on the ways.

Captain Coffin talked with the carpenters who were building his boats. Then he and Charles walked along the waterfront to Straight Wharf where the *John Jay* was moored.

Already the weather-beaten little ship had been turned on each side so that barnacles and seaweed could be scraped from her hull.

Next, her seams had been calked, or filled and smeared with hot tar. Now men were at work, painting her black, with white trim.

Nearby, riggers were swarming over the masts of the *Ranger*, fitting her out with new ropes. At the next wharf, stevedores were hoisting a new anchor to the deck of the whaling ship *Alliance*. And small boats were coming and going, as usual.

Leaving Charles on the wharf, Captain Coffin boarded the *John Jay* to inspect the painters' work. Then they crossed the wharf and entered the chandler's dark little shop.

The chandler sold compasses, spyglasses, tools, trypots, lanterns, brooms, axes, and many other articles which were used on the whaling ships. Zenas Coffin gave him a list of things which were needed for the *John Jay* and discussed prices with him. When he had finished, he and Charles started for the Coffins' counting house which was on Washington Street, near the warehouse.

This was Captain Coffin's office. In one corner there was a high, slant-topped desk, with a stool before it. Records and leather-bound account books were piled on a shelf. Charts, or marine maps, hung on the walls.

Zenas Coffin planned that some day, after Charles had been whaling, he would become a partner in the business. So he was just starting to teach him a little about it. Sometimes he gave him problems to solve, like what it would cost to outfit a whaleboat. At other times he gave him logbooks to read.

This reproduction of an actual page from an old whaler's logbook shows that two whales were caught on the first day, one on the second day, and that one whale was lost on the third day.

These were records, which were usually kept by the first mate, of the daily life aboard the ship on every voyage. The first mate wrote about the weather, the winds, and the position of the ship. He also told about whales. Often he did this by drawing small pictures, instead of using words. From the pictures, Charles learned to recognize the different kinds of whales and to tell at a glance which had escaped and which had been caught.

From the charts on the walls he learned the names of the oceans and seas which Nantucket men had explored, and the places where they had landed. Sometimes his father would point out where he thought the Coffins' ships might be, and Charles would hope that they were having greasy luck. But on that June day in 1810, one Nantucket ship was in trouble. The *Lydia*, with only half her oil casks filled, was on her way home.

6. A Flag at Half-Mast

On July 1, 1810, the *Lydia* returned. The news that a ship was approaching Nantucket spread, as usual, through the town. But no boys went racing to the captain's house to win a silver dollar. For the *Lydia's* flag was at half-mast, which meant that her captain was dead.

A sober crowd gathered at the wharf to meet the returning whalers. Dressed in their best shore clothes, the first and second mates went to the captain's home to tell his widow what had happened.

"Captain Swain killed by a whale."

That is all the record tells of how Captain
Silas Swain met his death. But many men
were killed by whales. Sometimes they were
drowned when a whale overturned or stove in
their boat. Often a whale crushed a boat and
her crew in its powerful jaws.

Once a fighting sperm whale seized a man
who was struggling in the water near a stove
boat and swam away with him. Another whale
grabbed a boat and shook it. Three of the
men were tossed into the air and the harpooner
fell back into the whale's mouth. The whale
carried him under water and then surfaced
and spat him out. When his shipmates pulled
him from the sea he was dead.

Some whaling men met with accidents which were not caused by whales. If a line attached to a harpooned whale had not been carefully coiled, it kinked. That kink could catch a man around the legs and he would be yanked under water before he had time to cry out. Men who were cutting blubber from dead whales sometimes slipped on the greasy decks, fell overboard, and were eaten by sharks.

Then there were storms! Bad storms with such strong gales that the whaling men said, "It's blowing so hard it takes two men to hold one man's hair on."

The wind roared. The ship rolled. And men who were furling the sails might be thrown into the raging ocean, or fall to the decks and be killed. Ships were sunk in these storms, too, and all aboard would be lost.

Whaling was such a dangerous business that there were many widows on Nantucket. As soon as news arrived of the death of a whaling man, friends and relatives hurried to his house to comfort his family. Then his widow began to plan how to earn money for herself and her children.

She might do sewing for other people, or work in one of the small candle factories. She might turn her front room into a school and teach children how to read and write. Or she might open a store in her house and sell needles, pins, hooks and eyes, scissors, thread, and homemade sweets.

Whatever she did, she would also have her own housework to do. Like most women on Nantucket, she must cook, and clean, and milk the cow. She must churn butter, make cheese, and salt down fish and pork.

She must wash the clothes in water which she brought from the well and heated in big pots over the fire. She must iron and make

her own soap. She must card and spin wool
or flax, weave it into cloth, and make clothing
and bedding for her family. She must knit
stockings and mittens, and doctor her children
when they were sick.

Some women whose husbands were away
whaling also had business to attend to. The
wife of a captain or shipowner often had to
order goods from cities on the mainland, or
from London. She had to keep the records and
account books straight and pay the bills.

In families where fathers had been lost at
sea or were away whaling, boys and girls
worked hard, too. Girls learned, before they

were ten, to help around the house, to knit, and to take care of the smaller children. Boys kept the water buckets filled and brought in wood for the fires. They fed the chickens and kept the cow shed clean. They gathered clams on the beaches for chowder and kept their families supplied with fish which they caught from the shore or from rowboats. Many Nantucket boys were excellent fishermen by the time they were ten and went off alone on short fishing trips.

Yet, in spite of all they had to do, the boys and girls had time for fun, and the women had time to go visiting. Because they were

lonely without their husbands, some women went visiting almost every afternoon.

Putting on her bonnet and shawl, a woman would walk to a friend's house to drink tea, eat little cakes, and talk. Since they were whalers' wives or widows, their conversation might run like this.

"Drop anchor and come aboard," a woman might say to a guest who was just arriving. "Has thee cleared thy decks already?"

"Yes, my house is shipshape. But little Mary blew up such a squall when I left that I was afraid I'd have to go back to port."

"Well, I told my Seth that if he teased his brother again I'd tar him and lash him to the mast until his father gets home."

"How long has thy husband been gone?"

"More than two years now. I pray that he's safe."

All over the island, women prayed for the safety of their husbands. And when at last the whaling men returned, their wives dreaded the day when they would set out on another voyage.

That day came in September for the wives of the captain and the crew of the *Ranger*. A new voyage was about to begin.

These men are trying whale blubber on shipboard.

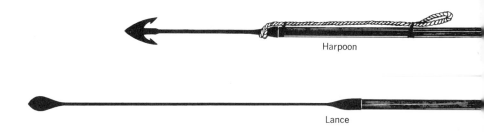

Harpoon

Lance

7. The *Ranger* Sails

"Oh, a ship she was rigged and ready for sea.
  Windy weather! Stormy weather!
  And all of her sailors were fishes to be.
  Blow ye winds westerly. Steady she goes."

It was the second week in September. The *Ranger* was rigged and almost ready for sea. Three new whaleboats had been swung on her davits, or cranes. Two extra boats were on a rack over the deck. A new brick tryworks had been built near her bow. Lances, harpoons, cutting spades, oars, and paddles were all in their places.

61

Now she was being loaded with food and other supplies. All day long, farmers' carts and warehouse drays rattled over the wharf, and stevedores struggled up the gangplank with barrels, boxes, and bags.

The stevedores carried scores of casks down into the hold. Some held fresh water. Some were empty. If the whalers were lucky, all would be brought back bursting with whale oil. And enough staves and hoops were put on the ship so that the cooper could make many more casks, as they were needed.

As for food, there were dozens of barrels of dried beef and pork, apples, flour, and molasses. Over three tons of hardtack, or ship's bread, were stowed away, as well as many bushels of peas, beans, potatoes, and big bags of tea and coffee.

Pots, kettles, and dishes were carried aboard. So were carpenters' tools, rolls of canvas, boards for repairing stove boats, and wood for fires under the try-pots and for cooking. There was also a big chest, called a slop chest, filled with new clothes and blankets which the whalers could buy when theirs were worn out.

Captain William Joy sat at a table on the deck with a list before him, checking off the supplies as they arrived. He had already signed up a crew of nineteen men and one boy, and had told them on what day the *Ranger* would leave.

On the day before the sailing, there was a feeling of bustle and excitement in the home of every crew member. Women took final stitches in new shirts and underwear, or hastily finished knitting mittens or stockings. Kitchens were filled with delicious odors as special food was cooked for the men who were going. And friends stopped in with small presents. There might be a bottle of homemade rhubarb and ginger syrup to cure a stomachache. Or quill pens for the first mate who kept the ship's record, or log. There might also be a new jackknife or some handkerchiefs or a loaf of fresh plum cake. Whatever it was, it was probably packed in the sea chest, and all of the sea chests were taken to the ship before dark.

It was the custom, before the whalers left, to have farewell parties on their last night ashore. Because many of the people were Quakers, they did not dance or sing or play cards at these social gatherings. They sat in comfortable kitchens and ate and talked.

The young men told about their adventures and described strange places they had seen. The girls served cold meats, puddings, pies, tarts, cakes, and hot chocolate or tea. At nine o'clock the curfew rang and the party ended.

There was usually some girl who did not want her young man to sail away the next day. So she put a black cat or kitten under a tub before she went to bed that night. This was supposed to cause such a strong head wind when the ship was ready to leave, that she could not get out of the harbor.

But no such head wind blew on the day the *Ranger* was to sail. Early in the morning, after the cows had been driven to pasture, the town crier left his house. Up one sandy street and down another he walked, ringing his bell and calling out his news:

"A fine day and a fair wind. The *Ranger* sails this morning."

Soon the *Ranger's* crew, with their families and friends, began to gather on Straight Wharf. They stood about in little groups, talking. Fathers told their children to be good. Wives begged their husbands to be careful. Husbands gave last-minute advice about such matters as selling the old cow or having the roof fixed while they were gone.

Captain Joy, looking very fine in his blue coat with silver buttons, surely urged his son, William, to take care of his mother and sisters. Then he boarded the ship, followed by the first mate who carried a large bag of letters.

These letters were for men on other whaling ships. Often Nantucket ships met far out at sea, thousands of miles from home. Then they were anchored, or they were hove-to, with their sails against the masts, so that they were barely moving. Boats were lowered and some of the men from one ship visited men on the other, to exchange news and letters.

Whalers who sailed around Cape Horn into the Pacific Ocean also had their own post office. This was a box, nailed to a tree on Charles Island, which is one of the Galapagos Islands. Every ship from Nantucket stopped at the island so that someone could leave letters in that mailbox. Every ship that was bound for Nantucket stopped so that the men could pick up their letters.

The letters were usually addressed like this:

John Jones, Boat Steerer

Ship Leo

Pacific Ocean

Often the news they contained was several months old. But the whaling men were glad to have any word from their families.

"Write to me," the men on Straight Wharf said to their wives and sweethearts. "Send a letter on the next ship that sails. Write often."

Then it was time to leave. Many hearts were heavy, but there was no weeping or kissing or hugging. For the Nantucket Quakers did not show in public what they were feeling.

The men boarded the ship. Ropes were cast off. Sails were set. And the *Ranger* moved slowly from the wharf.

"Good-bye!" called the people in the crowd. "Greasy luck! God keep thee safe! Good-bye!"

The *Ranger* might be gone for two or three years. She might meet with disaster at sea and never return. But many boys in Nantucket wished they were sailing aboard her. Indeed, almost every boy on the island planned to sign up as a cabin boy on some ship as soon as he could.

For every cabin boy knew he had a chance to become a harpooner some day, and then a boat steerer, a mate, and a captain. If he had greasy luck, he might even become a ship owner. But, best of all, he was sure that wherever he went, his life as a whaler would be exciting and filled with adventure.

AMERICAN FISHING SCENES.

8. Aboard a Whaling Ship

A whaler's life was filled with adventure and excitement. But it was also a hard life, filled with dangerous and unpleasant work.

The whaling ships were small. In 1810 they were less than 100 feet long. Since a great deal of storage space was needed for casks of oil, there was little room for the men.

The brick tryworks and the windlass for raising the anchor took up most of the space on the top deck, at the bow. The steering wheel, the galley where the meals were cooked, and the stairs to the officers' quarters below took up space at the stern.

The captain's little stateroom was below the

top deck, near the foot of the stairs. It held his bed, a chest of drawers, and his sea chest. He also had a small room which contained a sofa, a desk, some books, and a medicine chest.

The captain was responsible to the owners of the ship for the ship herself, and for all the men aboard her. He charted the ship's course. He gave the orders and punished any man who disobeyed them. He took care of any who were injured or ill. If a man's arm or leg was too badly hurt in an accident to be saved, it was the captain who cut it off. He pulled aching teeth, put on tourniquets to stop

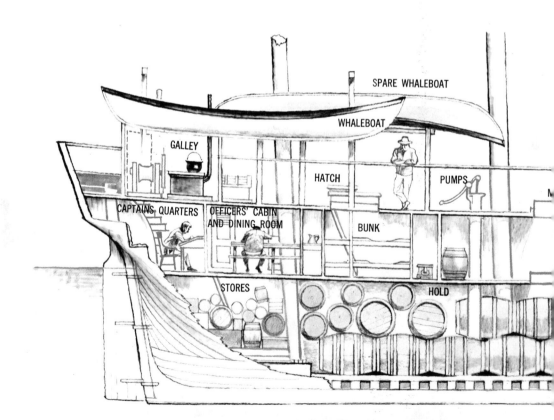

dangerous bleeding, and also doctored sick men.

The mates had quarters near the captain. They were in charge of the whaleboats and superintended the crew. They ate their meals with the captain in a tiny dining room.

The crew's quarters were in the bow of the ship. Two rows of short, narrow bunks, one above the other, lined the walls of a small room called the forecastle. In the middle of the forecastle there was a little table with a greasy whale oil lantern hanging over it. The sea chests, which were placed before each lower bunk, were the only seats.

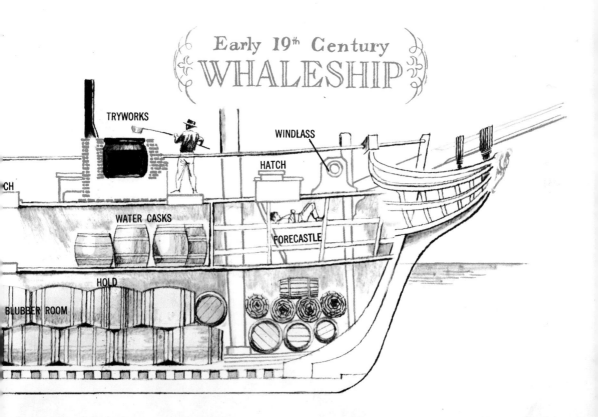

Early 19th Century
WHALESHIP

TRYWORKS

WINDLASS

HATCH

CH

WATER CASKS

FORECASTLE

HOLD

BLUBBER ROOM

The room was dark and smelly and so crowded that the men often crawled into the bunks to get out of the way. When the weather was bad they ate meals in the forecastle. When it was good, they ate on deck.

As soon as a meal was ready, the cook in the little galley called out the news. Then two or three men went to the galley to get tubs filled with food, and a bucket of tea or coffee sweetened with molasses. They carried these to the deck or the forecastle. The other men rushed to fill their tin pans and cups.

Usually the tubs contained boiled salt beef or pork, mixed with hardtack. But two or three times a week there was lobscouse. This was made of salted meat, potatoes or dried beans, and hardtack, boiled together in a stew.

For dessert the men were often given a baked pudding, called dandy funk, which was made of powdered hardtack, lard, water, and molasses. As a special treat they had duff. To make duff, the cook stirred flour and lard with dried apples or raisins. Then he boiled the mixture in a bag and served it with molasses.

Once in a while the captain was able to stop at a port or an island where he could get fresh meat, chickens, vegetables and fruit. Then his men had a feast. But usually the whalers' food was very poor.

Sometimes their pay was poor, too. Whaling men were never paid regular wages. Instead, everyone from the captain to the cabin boy received a share of the profits from each voyage. These shares were called lays. The captain's lay was the largest and the cabin boy's was the smallest. The lays of the rest of the crew were in between.

If the men had hard luck and caught few whales, the pay for everyone was poor. But if their luck was greasy and many whales were killed, everyone made money.

Catching a whale and killing it was an exciting and dangerous sport. Stripping off the blubber and trying out the oil was hard, disgusting, dirty work.

When the dead whale had been towed to the ship, it was made fast to the right, or starboard side, with chains. Then a platform of planks, called a cutting-in stage, was swung over the ship's side. The captain and the first mate climbed out on it. With the help of some other men, they cut the whale's huge head from its body and divided it into three sections.

A crewman bails oil from
the "case" of a whale
with a bucket carried on
a pulley rope.

If it was the head of a sperm whale, one
section, called the case, was full of pure
sperm oil. Sometimes this case was too heavy
to be hauled aboard the ship. Then a man
was lowered into it, to bail out the oil with a
bucket.

Another section of the head, called the junk,
held oil and spermaceti. The third section was
the jaw, containing the teeth, which the whalers
used for scrimshaw.

When the three sections had been hoisted to the deck, the second mate climbed to the cutting stage. With a sharp spade, he cut the blubber on the whale's body into strips. The men on deck hauled the strips aboard with strong blubber hooks and tackle, and lowered them into the blubber room. There, other men cut the strips into chunks about 14 inches square. These chunks were taken on deck, where two men sliced into them again and again with a sharp, two-handled knife, and then threw them into the try-pots.

As the crewmen cut the blubber, a huge hook pulls it aboard the ship.

Meanwhile, hot fires had been lighted in the brick stoves under the pots. The blubber sizzled and crackled as it boiled into oil, sending black smoke high into the air. When the oil was ready, it was ladled into casks and more blubber was put into the pots.

This work went on for many hours. By the time it was over, the ship's deck was covered with grease and blood, and so were the men. As soon as the last cask had been stowed away in the hold, the men scrubbed the ship and themselves. Then they waited for the lookout to sight another whale.

Sometimes a ship cruised for many days before the lookout shouted, "There she blows!" During this time the crew had little to do. They scrimshawed and patched their clothes and scanned the ocean, hoping to see another ship. Sometimes they did. She might be from New Bedford, Massachusetts or from one of the other small whaling centers. But in 1810 she was usually from Nantucket.

When the two ships had come close together, they were hove-to. Then the men began to visit back and forth in their whaling boats. They called this gamming. Often a gam lasted for almost a week. The whalers ate together,

played jokes on one another, and danced together. They sang whaling songs and told stories of their adventures. They exchanged letters, if they had any, and talked about their families.

The gam went on until the captains decided it should end. Then good-byes were said, sails were raised, and each ship went her own way.

On both ships the whalers hoped for a gam with another ship soon. And they looked forward to the day when all their casks were full of oil, and the captain gave the order to start home.

9. Lessons, Games, and Stories

Soon after the *Ranger* left Nantucket in September, the *John Jay* sailed away. Then the *Renown* returned from the Indian Ocean, loaded with oil. As the days grew shorter and the wild ducks on the ponds flew south, a few more whaling ships came and went.

Schooners from the mainland brought firewood and other supplies which the islanders would need in the winter. Men piled dried seaweed around their houses to keep out the chilly winds. In the mornings, children dashed from their cold bedrooms to dress before kitchen fires. They ate big breakfasts of hot corn-meal mush, swimming in milk and covered with molasses. Then they bundled up in coats or cloaks, caps or bonnets, and mittens and started off to school.

Sometimes it was so foggy they could hardly see where they were going, or the wind was blowing almost hard enough to knock them down. But bad weather seldom kept the children of whaling families at home.

In 1810 there were no free schools on Nantucket, so most of the children went to dame schools. These schools were taught by widows of whaling men, or by other women who wanted to earn money. Some of the

A young boy learns the craft of sailmaking.

schools were called cent schools because the teacher only charged a cent a day.

The boys and girls studied together. Sitting on hard benches in someone's made-over parlor or bedroom, they learned to read, write, spell, do arithmetic, and sew. Even the boys learned to sew so that they could mend sails and patch clothes when they went whaling.

The children usually studied in dame schools until they were eleven or twelve. Then boys who wanted to go on learning from books went to the little grammar school near Mill Hill. Some of the other boys became fishermen. The rest were apprenticed to ropemakers, blacksmiths, sailmakers, coopers, and other men who were making things for whaling ships.

An apprentice ran errands, kept his master's workshop clean and did other odd jobs. In return for this, his master taught him his trade. On Nantucket almost all boys, rich or poor, learned trades. For whaling was an uncertain business, and they must be prepared to make a living in another way, if they should ever need to.

When girls left school, they learned from their mothers how to cook and run a house. Some girls also learned to manage a small business and keep accounts. Others learned dressmaking. Even the daughters of wealthy shipowners were taught some way of earning money. Then they could support themselves later on, if their whaling husbands were killed or lost at sea.

Yet life was not all work and no play for the children of Nantucket. The girls played with their dolls, and had games of hopscotch, tag, and hide-and-go-seek. The boys swam, ran races on the beaches, and sailed home-made boats on the ponds. They kicked around a blown-up hog's bladder in a game they called kickpoke, and flew kites on Mill Hill.

In the summer, both girls and boys went on
berrying parties, and on picnics which they
called squantums. They gathered ripe beach
plums and wild grapes in the fall. In winter
they skated on the ice-covered ponds, and slid
down snowy hills on homemade sleds. And,
winter or summer, they were always ready to
listen to the stories which old whaling men
had to tell of their adventures.

What fun it must have been, on a winter's night, to sit before a blazing fire, listening to one of these stories. Rain or snow might be beating against the windows, and a gale might be blowing outside. But the kitchen was warm and snug, and the pounding of the surf sounded far, far away.

"Tell about pirates," some child might beg.

So there would be an exciting story about pirates who boarded a whaling ship and were killed by the brave men of her crew.

An artist drew this fanciful picture of a friendly whale resting on an ice floe while whaling crews hunt nearby.

Before another fire, someone else might be telling how he and his shipmates escaped from cannibals who wanted to kill and eat them.

There were stories of landing on beautiful islands and meeting friendly natives. And there were stories of other natives who attacked the whalers with spears tipped with sharks' teeth.

Volcanoes which erupted in fiery steam, high mountains, glittering icebergs, strange animals and birds—all came into these stories, too.

A Scale of 27 Feet.

"Did you know that some whales can sing?" one old whaler might begin.

Or a gray-haired captain might say quietly, "Tonight I'll tell you how an angry sperm whale rammed his head against our ship until he sank her."

There were very few story books in Nantucket, and the children listened wide-eyed to these tales of adventure and courage. When the stories were over, the boys were more eager than ever to go whaling some day. And each girl was sure she could never marry anyone except a brave whaling man.

10. Many Changes

"So be cheery, my lads,
  Let your hearts never fail,
  While the bold harpooner
  Is striking the whale."

Month after month, Nantucket men continued to hunt and kill whales. Then, in 1812, the United States went to war with England. The war began because English sea captains were kidnapping the sailors from American ships to serve in the English navy. It lasted more than two years.

During that time, all but twenty-three of Nantucket's whaling ships were captured or sunk. Almost no oil was brought to the island.

Tryhouses, candle factories, and shops were closed. Hundreds of men had no jobs, and many people were hungry.

But after the war ended, Nantucket became more prosperous than ever. Within a few years, new whaling ships were launched. The air rang again with the sound of hammers, the voices of stevedores and lighter-men, and the rattle of drays carrying casks of oil from the wharves.

Merchants and shipowners opened new warehouses and factories. They had the sandy main

A new fleet of whalers is being built after the great destruction of American ships in the War of 1812.

These fine houses were built in Nantucket's golden age.

streets paved with cobblestones, and built another wharf. Some of them made so much money that they built handsome new homes for their families, and times were good for everyone on the island.

Times were good in New Bedford, too, and in the smaller whaling ports. For America was growing rapidly and many thousands of people now wanted whale oil and candles. Soon there were so many whaling ships at sea that whales became hard to find. Captains had to cruise about three or four years before they had a full cargo of oil.

Larger ships were built for these long voyages and larger crews were needed to man them. Nantucket captains usually had no trouble in signing up enough good crewmen on the island. But other captains often had to advertise for men in the cities and towns along the coast. Most of the men who answered these advertisements were rough young fellows who knew nothing about whales or boats. So the captains had to train them after their ships were at sea. This brought changes into the life aboard many whaling ships, and the large ships, themselves, brought changes to Nantucket.

The sandbar, lying under water, still blocked the entrance to the harbor. The big new ships could not cross the bar, even after they were lightened. Before they sailed again, everything needed for the next voyage had to be taken out to them on lighters or small boats. This became more and more expensive. Nantucket shipowners began to lose money and to send out fewer ships each year. Before many years had passed, New Bedford, with a fine open harbor, had become the leading whaling center in the country.

They carried on a thriving business until, in

Large whaling ships could be towed over the sand bar
in Nantucket Harbor by a floating drydock or "camel"
in the years 1840 to 1849.

1859, someone discovered how to make
kerosene from mineral oil which was taken
from the ground in Pennsylvania. Kerosene
lamps gave a cheaper, brighter light than
whale oil lamps. And the great days of
whaling were over.

Yet the Nantucket whalers should not be
forgotten. They brought light and cheer into
the homes of thousands of Americans, living
long ago. It was their whale oil in lighthouse
lamps which, year after year, guided ships at
night.

Ice floes drift about whaling ships in the far north.

In their hunt for whales, they sailed fearlessly into unknown seas. They visited strange countries and discovered thirty islands which had never before been seen by white men. They crossed dangerous reefs and shoals. Carefully they made charts, showing where they had been and what they had found. They shared this information generously with other whalers, and with traders and explorers. In this way they helped Americans learn more about the world in which they lived.

Whaling is being done again today, mostly by Norwegians and Englishmen. Whale oil is used in making paints and varnishes and in

A whaling ship rests at an island in the South Seas.

lubricating fine machinery in many countries. The bones of whales are ground up and mixed with food for chicken and cattle. Whale meat is eaten in Japan.

Now the whalers travel on steamships which are like small factories. They chase whales in speedy boats, and shoot them with grenade guns. They can kill several whales in one day and their business is good.

But no joyful cry of "There she blows!" rings out from the masthead. And no one ashore calls when they leave port, "Greasy luck! God keep thee safe!" as mothers, wives and children called when Nantucket men went whaling.

Glossary

blubber: the fat of whales and other large sea mammals

blubber hook: a tool used to haul strips of blubber on board ship

case: a cavity in the head of a sperm whale which contains a fine pure oil

casks: barrels in which whale oil is stored

chandler: a seller of supplies for whaling ships

cooper: a barrel-maker

counting house: the office where a merchant keeps his books and carries on his business

cutting spade: a tool used to cut blubber into strips

cutting-in stage: a platform hanging at the side of the whaling ship on which men stand to cut whale blubber

davit: a crane used for lowering or raising whaleboats over the side of a ship

dray: a two-wheeled wagon or cart without fixed sides

duck trousers: trousers made of a strong cotton material called duck

forecastle: the forward part of a ship where the men live

galley: a ship's kitchen

gam: a visit between the crews of two whaling ships at sea

hardtack: a hard bread made of flour and water without salt

harpoon: a barbed spear used in capturing whales

hoops: circular iron strips used to hold together the sides of casks

hove to: a ship with sails arranged so that the ship cannot move away

lance: a spear used in killing whales

lay: a share of the profits from a voyage

lighter: a large barge used in loading or unloading ships

logbook: a record of daily life aboard a ship

pea jacket: a heavy woolen jacket worn by sailors

schooner: a large sailing ship

scrimshaw: carved objects made by whaling men from whalebone

slop chest: a chest in which clothing is kept, to be sold to members of the crew

spermaceti: a waxy solid taken from the oil of sperm whales

squantum: a Nantucket picnic

starboard: the right side of a ship

staves: narrow strips of wood which form the sides of a cask

stevedores: men who load and unload ships in port

stove boat: a boat which has been smashed in

tryhouse: a long shed where blubber oil is refined

try-pot: a metal pot in which blubber is melted into oil

tryworks: a brick furnace into which try-pots are placed

whale: a mammal which lives in the sea and looks like a fish

whalebone: a hornlike material which grows like a fringe from the right whale's upper jaw and strains its food

Index